12 TIPS ON FINANCE

12 TIPS ON FINANCE

Herbert N. Casson

Tynron Press
England

© Herbert N. Casson
Tynron Press, 1992

This revised and updated edition published in 1992 by
Tynron Press
Unit 3 Turnpike Close
Lutterworth
Leicestershire LE17 4JA
England

ISBN 1-85646-075-4

Cover designed by K.H. Teo
Typeset by System Set Services, Singapore
Printed in Singapore by Kin Keong Printing Co. Pte Ltd

CONTENTS

Foreword

Introduction

Foreword

This is the third edition of this book. It has been published in eight countries and has been generally accepted as a standard book on how to invest money safely. It has been bought by brokers, bankers and speculators.

This book gives a few rules and methods that many wise and successful investors have used, and that may save you from losing your hard-earned savings. It gives at least a dozen ways of preventing losses in the investment of money.

It does not advise anyone to speculate. This book is not a tout for any Stock Exchange. But millions of people do speculate, and before they do so, they should know some of the rules of the game.

Introduction

This book is like a sharp-edged tool - it is not for children or weaklings. It is not to be glanced at or skimmed through in a hurry. It is to be studied carefully and considered as a whole. My purpose in writing it is to give my readers as much practical help as possible, not only in the art of making money, but also in the art of investing it.

As you will see, this book is quite unique. There is no other book of its kind in any library. It is the result of nearly 30 years' experience in and around the Stock Exchange. It contains not only my own dearly bought experience, but much that I learnt from others who were wiser. Nothing in it has been taken from books or from any educational institution. It deals with those practical, personal matters learnt at first hand.

The truth is that in the world of finance all of us make so many mistakes that no one dares to call himself an authority on the subject. There is no such thing as absolute truth and absolute safety, so people muddle along in the best way they can and parents give very little guidance to their children. Every new generation makes the same old mistakes.

There are not as many "axioms" in Finance as there are in Business and Mathematics, but there are certainly a few "Tips", and I am offering 12 of them for the benefit of people who have saved money and who do not want to lose it.

Surveys show that out of every 100 people in business, perhaps only four become rich and keep their money. Most of them make money but lose it. People in business make money up to the age of 50, then begin to lose it. Why? Is it not because they have learned the art of business - which is money-making - but not the art of finance - which is money-keeping?

So, in the following chapters you will find enough information about personal finance to prevent you from losing your money. More than this, you will find in the last chapter a definite system of investment. It will help you to make your money work and earn more.

I do not promise that you will make big profits; I do not even advise you to do so. I made 18 per cent profits, tax free, by using this system, which at least proves that it is worthy of any person's serious attention.

This book is written only for the efficient few who have the sense, courage and integrity to put the information in it to good use.

Herbert N. Casson

Tip No. 1

BUY ONLY WHAT YOU KNOW

Almost all business people buy rubbish when they begin to invest their money. Invariably, they buy shares in a business they know nothing about.

Beginners in the world of finance want to make big profits. They scorn six or seven per cent. They want 15 per cent and even set their sights on 20 per cent. They want perfection, and as perfection is seldom to be found close to home, they invest their money in properties 10,000 miles away. This could account for the sale of so much mining stock and securities in countries far away.

In a nutshell, every amateur investor is more or less a rainbow-chaser. Even the most practical grocer or factory manager will invest his first £1,000 in worthless securities put out by either dreamers or rascals and based on some worthless jungle project in Africa or some dishonest organisation in South America or the Balkans. Many elderly people probably have small bundles of such so-called "securities" tucked away in their safes or cupboards. The only valuable things in the bundles are the strings they are tied up with. They bought what they knew nothing about and paid the price for their folly.

1

As I intend to tell the blunt truth in this series of TWELVE TIPS, I have to say that the world of finance is not as honest as the world of trade and commerce. You will find the ablest and the most trustworthy people in the world of finance at the top. This is true in every business community. You will find, however, a horde of the most unprincipled swindlers in finance at the bottom. Most of them act within the law. Many are church-goers and appear to lead exemplary lives. But they are more dangerous to the public than all the burglars and pickpockets combined.

If a manufacturer passes off tap water as mineral water, he can be dragged before a judge and fined. But a financier can sell liabilities as assets all year long, and the law takes off its hat to him.

In finance you should never believe everything you hear. You must have the attitude of Descartes: you must *doubt everything*. A tip is merely an opinion. Often, it is a lie with a purpose. In nine cases out of ten, the tips to buy come from the sellers, and the tips to sell come from the buyers.

In finance, ten lies are born every minute. Most of them are not wicked lies - merely what we might call financial inexactitudes but they serve the purpose of making people lose their money just as much as though they were outright swindles.

In finance there are no disinterested people. Everybody has an axe to grind. Everyone is trying to push prices either up or down. Not even the Recording Angel could expect truth from people in such circumstances.

As for prospectuses they are not much better than tips. There are clever wordtwisters who can write a prospectus on a wheelbarrow and make it look like a Rolls Royce. Leaflets and circulars are almost always just about as true as the tale of Robinson Crusoe. There is generally a basis of fact and a wonderful super-structure of pure imagination. Advertisements are usually more reliable than leaflets and prospectuses, but it is better to take note of what the Financial Editor says than to believe the advertisement.

Balance sheets are still more reliable, but it is a fact that losses are cooked up to show gains, and *vice versa*, in thousands of balance sheets every year. Bear in mind that a printer will print anything and ask no questions. So will many newspapers and magazines. The main difference between the spoken lie and the printed lie is that the latter appears more plausible.

BUY ONLY WHAT YOU KNOW. If you are a grocer, put your money into the shares of the best company that sells you goods. If you know about railways, put your money into the stocks and debentures of the railway that is managed most wisely. If you are a builder, buy land. If you are a seasoned traveller, buy airline or shipping shares. If you know nothing of trade and commerce, buy Government securities.

In all cases, whenever you can, buy an interest in a business that is nearby. Invest in your own town. Buy what you can see. Far-off fields look green, but they are not half so green as you are if you invest your good money in them.

3

First, buy the house you live in. Then buy the house next door. The experience that you will get as a landlord will soon cure you of rainbow-chasing. If there is no property nearby that you can put your money into, then buy the securities of those well-known firms that have been carrying on business for 30 years or longer. Any company that has paid dividends for 30 years is as good a risk as anything can be in this world of risks.

But always invest, if possible, in a business that you know about. The trade that you know about is the one where you are least likely to get fooled in. You must not be a greenhorn when you invest. You must not be credulous. Ignorance is dangerous, especially in finance. If you stick to what you know, you are likely to stick to your money.

Of all gambles, the most risky is betting on a horse race. Nobody knows what the outcome of a race will be except when it is a predetermined fraud. There are so many variables in both horses and jockeys that no one can be absolutely sure in a fair race who the winner will be.

There are many gambles in finance that are almost as uncertain as horse racing. Most gold mines and many copper mines are only slightly better than the Derby as a means of doubling your money. More money is invested in gold mines than is taken out of them. Every £100 invested in gold mines has cost L115. There are more losers than winners.

So, in finance, which I would define as "the art of keeping your money and making it earn more", the first rule is to put your money in what you know yourself, not what anyone tells you. Once a person has money, very few people will tell him the truth. All manner of people, respectable and disreputable, will set out to do their best to take it away from him. As a rule, it is harder to keep money than to make it. Consequently, the first Tip is: Be careful. Buy only what you know.

Tip No. 2

Never Buy Under Pressure

This Tip holds good in both business and finance. Every person who has some money tucked away should make a solemn pledge never to spend, lend or invest it under pressure.

There are so many rogues, greedy relatives and not-so-needy beggars in the world that people with money must turn themselves into impregnable "forts". They must not allow themselves to be "assaulted". They must always be on their guard against the parasites who live by persuading other people to part with their money.

When you are asked for money, always postpone your answer - this is the golden rule that could prevent you from losing it. There are so many persuasive people in the world that it is hard for a person to keep what he has. The art of getting other people to part with their money has been developed to a high degree by parasites, swindlers, and no less by governments.

The art of *attack* has been much more developed than the art of *defence*. That is why I am writing this book - to build up, for the first time, an art of defence.

In the world of finance there are always clever rascals who can separate you from your money without using force. I know of a man who has taken more money from people than have scores of burglars put together. He floated 45 "companies" in 21 years. These "companies" had, on paper, a capital of about £150,000,000. Most of them collapsed overnight like balloons. They were not companies at all - they were swindles.

There are still plenty of swindlers around. They are in every town and city. They don't earn money, they simply transfer it. They concoct wonderful schemes. They rush about in great excitement and shout: "Wonderful scheme! Make millions! Who wants plenty of money? Quick! Come and get the money!"

This sort of thing always draws a crowd. People who are quite sensible in other matters will give these swindlers their money and in many cases, it is their hard-earned savings. After a few months, the cheats disappear with all the money and the people are left with worthless schemes. It seems there are not enough laws to prevent people from being swindled. It is quite possible for even a known swindler to relieve people of a great deal of money in the name of some so-called "safe" investment scheme.

There is no limit to either credulity or audacity in the world of finance. Your friends and even your own flesh and blood - will apply themselves diligently to the task of transferring your money from your pocket to theirs. Just as trees in the jungle are weakened and pulled down by poison ivy, so people in business are also weakened by the human ivy that clings to them and pulls them down.

Consequently, there must be a system of *self-defence* in the matter of finance. Those who want to keep or spend their own money must learn to protect themselves. They must never surrender when they are attacked. They must think coolly and quietly to themselves: "What will I get? How do I know I will get it?"

Self-interest is not an ignoble thing. It has only been called ignoble by predatory parasites who live on other people's generosity. Self-interest is a structural virtue. It is one of the pillars that hold up the whole edifice of civilisation. The philosophy of credulity and selflessness was invented by beggars, and it has been constantly used by thieves. The more dupes, the more thieves. "Thou shalt not steal," says one of Ten Commandments. But this is only half the law. It should have been completed by adding "and thou shalt not be stolen from."

Once a man owns something, he must keep a level head and talk the matter over with his wife. A woman is less credulous than a man in money matters. She is more suspicious. She would sooner have a bird in her hand than two in the bush.

A woman is usually keener to make or get money and surer to keep it. A man tends to enjoy life, but a woman thinks more of the things she can get out of it. Therefore, every man should avail himself of the advice of his wife or mother on all matters pertaining to investments.

There is no good reason why you should give people your money just because you cannot get the better of them in an argument or disprove their claims. Neither should you part with your money because you find yourself overpowered by the force of their personalities. The only reason you should sign a cheque is because you are definitely going to get full value for the amount stated on the cheque.

Do not participate in anything risky unless you belong to Lloyds of London. The Lloyds brokers know the fair market price of risks, and you don't. When someone dashes into your office and says: "Quick! Sign a cheque for £50,000 and give it to me. We can buy Kingsway if we act at once!", tell him quietly that he can have it all to himself as he saw the opportunity first. And call his attention to a sign on your desk which says: "What I have, I hold."

No matter if you can buy a bank for a piece of cheese; don't give away a good piece of cheese. When a person says, "Now or never", say "Never". In finance, always be suspicious of speed and urgency, unless you yourself have discovered good reasons for acting quickly. Once in a while, you may lose a golden opportunity by waiting till tomorrow, but in the long run you will have more money and fewer regrets.

When you are minding your own affairs and playing your own game, be as quick as you can; but when you are parting with money or property, go slow. *Never buy, give, lend or invest under pressure. You may easily lose in a minute the savings of a year or even a lifetime.*

Tip No. 3

Speculate on Properties, Not Schemes

In the world of finance, everyone speculates. All take risks. All back their judgments, and either win or lose.

Finance consists of investment and speculation, and the cleverest banker in the world cannot tell you where one ends and the other begins. Many an investment has turned into a speculation overnight, and many a speculation has ripened into an investment.

One of the main risks in the realm of finance is that an honest and optimistic builder of businesses may in a slump suddenly find himself in prison. Every financier is a *trustee* and is responsible in law for the successful handling of other people's money entrusted to him or her. And the line between safety and risk is so finely drawn that it is difficult to tell the difference between them.

All business-builders must take risks. They must speculate and guess what is going to turn up in the future. There is no infallible rule by which they can play safe, but there are a few guidelines to show them the danger spots - and one of them is: speculate on properties, not schemes.

You may ask: "What is the difference between a property and

a scheme?" The answer is that a property is anything that has intrinsic value, while a scheme depends for its value entirely on the way in which it is carried out.

A property is tangible; you can always sell it, if you wish, in a week or two. But a scheme is only an idea. It has no existence in the material world. Any property, however old and dilapidated, has a money value, but the most perfect scheme may not be worth the paper it is drawn up on. It could be just a door to bankruptcy.

Now, it is a peculiarity of human nature that most people prefer a scheme to property. The reason, probably, is that a scheme is always perfect. It has no past mistakes. It is spick and span. It "can't fail". It is as faultless as a rainbow, and very similar. A scheme appeals to the imagination. It takes the mind away from all details of cost and management. It deals with hopes and desires and optimism, not with facts, difficulties and losses. A scheme tells people what they want to believe, not what they ought to believe. Consequently, schemes are always popular. The same old swindles spring up again and again. Every new generation will always throw away money on worthless gold mines, oil wells and ranches.

Not that I would have schemes made illegal - far from it. The Bank of England was once a scheme. So was Lloyds of London. Both have survived for more than two centuries and are still going strong. The Bank of England was incorporated by Royal Charter in 1694, and Lloyd's, with more than 31,000 underwriting members and premium income worth £6,000 million a year, evolved during the 18th century from dealings at Lloyd's Coffee House and was incorporated by Act of Parliament in 1871.

My point is that investing in schemes is for those who can afford it. It is not for people of small means and little experience. The percentage of failures is too high, very likely 50 to 1. None but the rich should back a new scheme, and even then they should put only a small percentage of their capital in it. Not more than 20 per cent of any person's money should be invested in a scheme.

Schemes are of all sorts - good, bad and indifferent. They are put forward by the best - and the worst - people. Some past schemes are now strong, reliable companies. Most failed long ago. Often, the schemes of honest men go wrong, and the schemes of swindlers turn into solid, permanent businesses.

There is no sure way of telling a good scheme from a bad one, when it is first launched. All you can do, if you don't want to lose your money, is to keep out of schemes altogether, and put your money into properties. A property can depreciate, but it cannot disappear into thin air, as a scheme is apt to do. By good planning and salesmanship, a property can always be turned into money. Or it can be developed into a paying business.

Usually, a new enterprise is part property and part scheme. This mixing up of the real and the unreal fools most people. It fooled Farrow, the founder of Farrow's bank, for instance. He was not a financier. He never knew the difference between a property and a scheme. He would buy a quarry for £20,000, tie it up to a scheme, and capitalise the two for £100,000. That was the main reason for his failure.

Every business enterprise consists, more or less, of property and a scheme, but the danger comes in when the scheme is too big for the property.

A sound business is like a pyramid, smaller at the top than at the base, and a dangerous business is like an inverted pyramid. It is top-heavy. It has *too much scheme.*

The basic difference between a property and a scheme, is that a property retains its value, no matter who owns it; while a scheme is entirely a matter of honesty and good management.

The cleverer a man is, the more he can depend on schemes. The duller he is, the more he should depend on properties. This is blunt advice, but it would have saved a lot of people from losing their money in recent years. Sparrows should not fly too high. They should not try to be eagles. At any rate, they should first try themselves out, and find out whether they are eagles or sparrows.

There is a time for caution in finance, as well as a time for courage, and the first rule is always - *learn the facts about the scheme, the property and yourself.* This Tip does not apply to the strong, experienced, self-reliant financier, who has prospered for years in the jungle of finance. Even he gets caught at times by schemes that are all hot air; but in the main he is able to protect himself. Very often, he will beat the schemer at his own game.

This Tip is meant more for the person who is not a financier - for the businessman or professional who has a little money to invest. People should not try to run before they can walk. They should never invest in schemes until they have had at least ten years' experience with properties. Those people who have had experience with properties are not so likely to be fooled by empty talk and promises. People who know about houses and land and factories are not so likely to chase rainbows.

The important thing to remember is that a scheme in itself is nothing. It is only a quick way of spending your money, unless there is someone at the back of the scheme who has enough experience and ability and honesty to make a success of it.

Tip No. 4

Buy Only What Can Be Resold

Don't get stuck with something you can't sell. Many people in business have more than once forgotten this important rule and made losses; thousands have lost their savings in the same way.

Don't buy a thing just because it pleases you, unless you are rich enough to lose your money and not mind it. Many people make this mistake in the beginning. They buy goods that they fancy and then discover that they suit nobody else. So the goods remain on their shelves - a dead loss to them.

People also make this mistake in buying land or houses. They go to some out-of-the-way place and build a house. Five years later, when they try to sell the house, they find that nobody wants it. It has no market value at all, so they must either sell it for a song or wait for years to find a foolish buyer.

In almost every county, you will find an odd, dilapidated house sitting alone on top of a hill. "Smith's Folly" cost £100,000 to build, but it was sold for £8,000. Smith, who built a house with hardly any resale value, obviously forgot this fourth Tip.

One Londoner, more artistically inclined than business-minded, built a bungalow in a remote part of Surrey. He built it when costs were at their peak, and spent most of his money on it - more than £240,000. It was designed to please himself, with a thatched roof and parquet floors and stained glass windows. I saw it advertised in a Sunday paper: "For Sale - £120,000". He will probably accept £90,000 for it - losing £150,000 because he forgot this fourth Tip.

Another Londoner who had saved £20,000 bought shares in a local company - a small manufacturing business. The shares were possibly worth as much as he paid for them, but the price dropped drastically and he could not find a buyer at the price he wanted for them. He is faced with two choices: he must either sell at a loss or hold on to the shares indefinitely.

Another businessman bought the patent of a machine. If the patent was not infringed, if the machine could be made cheaply, and if there was a demand for it, he could have made a fortune. But he forgot these three "ifs" when he bought the patent. When he wanted to sell, nobody wanted to buy. And so it goes on. There are thousands of such cases. People make this mistake all the time - they buy what they cannot sell.

Always, in buying, there are several factors to bear in mind:

1. You may change your mind. The house that pleases you today may displease you tomorrow, or displease your wife - which is even more likely and serious.
2. Price is controlled by demand, not by cost or value. Price is what somebody will give for it. Last month I saw an aerodrome sold for £38,000 and a postage stamp for

£100,000.

3. You should not spend money on a whim, and deceive yourself that it is an investment. Buy to please yourself - yes - but not unless you can afford to throw away the money.

4. The more unique and abnormal a property is, the less likely you are to find a purchaser. The more ordinary and commonplace a thing is, the greater the crowd of buyers.

Ordinary people want ordinary things, and nine-tenths of the people in the world are ordinary. Too many people forget this. The more peculiar and original and personal a thing is, the more you will lose when you sell it. This is a fact that artistic people never seem to understand, and that many business people are liable to overlook when they buy something.

To put it another way, we may say that goods should be as much like money as possible from the point of view of finance. The great value of money is that *everybody wants it*. You can always exchange money for goods.

If you buy Shell shares, for instance, you can sell them at any time. You can sell them through the Stock Exchange in ten seconds. This shows that Shell shares are nearly as saleable as money. They have the advantage of paying high dividends. But if you buy shares in an unknown oil company, you may offer them for sale in vain. Nobody wants them. You're stuck.

Now, the unknown oil company's shares may be just as good *value* as the Shell shares, but they are not known and therefore not wanted. There is no market for them and they are therefore not worth so much. You must sell them at a low price or not at all.

Suppose that both oil companies paid 30 per cent dividends, free of tax. The well-known company's shares would be worth at least five times their face value, while the unknown company's shares would be worth only four times their face value. There should be a discount of at least 20 per cent on any shares or property that cannot be sold quickly.

Saleability is an element of value. This is a maxim that will make you more money when you sell, and save you more money when you buy. Behind this Tip lies the tremendous factor of goodwill, and behind goodwill lies publicity. Here we see the cost of oblivion - there is no market for the things that nobody knows about.

Especially at the present time, this Tip is of the highest value to every business, whether small or big. You should not tie up your money in goods that cannot be sold quickly. You should buy only those goods that you can turn into money quickly and without losses. This is the ideal that few of us can reach. But the nearer you are to it, the further you are from bankruptcy.

Business, as a process, consists in changing goods into money and money into goods. Goods - money - goods - money. If you make a profit on each exchange, that is business. If you don't make a profit, then it is not business. It is failure. Consequently, when you buy anything, you should ask yourself: "Is the price likely to rise, and are there other people who want it?" If so, then you can buy safely.

If you want to see this Tip illustrated in a dramatic way, go to an auction sale and notice the immense differences in the prices obtained. A handsome table is put up. Everybody wants a table. Twelve people bid against each other. The table is knocked down for £95. Its real value is £80. Next, a large glass mirror, of peculiar shape, is put up. Only two people bid. It goes for £15, although it cost £160 to make. Then, a large oil painting of the seller himself is put up. Nobody wants it. Everybody laughs. The auctioneer gives it away to a buyer who strenuously objects. Yet it cost the seller £400 to have it painted two years ago.

So, a part of the value of every property depends upon its saleability. Unless you have money to lose, buy only what can be quickly resold without a loss.

Tip No. 5

Take Your Profit

"I'm sorry I didn't sell it when I had the chance." How often have you heard people say this? Very likely, you have said it yourself.

Prices soared in 1918 and 1928. And 59 years later, on 16 October 1987, the Financial Times/Stock Exchange 100 Share Index peaked at 2,443.4 points. On 19 October (Black Monday) the index dropped a hefty 250.7 points to 1,801.6 points, resulting in a 94.3 billion drop in aggregate share value to 354.747 billion. It picked up 142.2 on 21 October, then fell again in the next two days to close even lower at 1,795.2 points. A little over a year later, the total market value of UK equities was 398.669 billion. The few who were wise sold out in 1918, 1928 and before Black Monday in 1987. The foolish were those who bought.

Most people invariably buy when prices are high. They always have and probably always will. They buy when everybody else is buying. Many who could have sold at those times probably refused to do so. If they had sold their property or shares, they could have bought them back in 1920, 1930 or when the Stock Market took that nose-dive in 1987, at possibly half the price they sold them for.

A man with £20,000 worth of property, for instance, could have sold out for £200,000 and could have bought it back again for £100,000. He would still have his property, with £100,000 more on top of it.

Several wise old shipowners sold their ships in 1918. A few years later, they could have bought the same ships back again for much less than the amount they got for selling them. The most recent severe decline in ship prices was between 1984 and 1986. The price of some types of ships during this period fell from £24 million to £7 million. After 1986, prices generally began to rise. Sometimes there is far more profit to be made out of selling and buying ships than in operating them.

This is just the point I want to make clear - that in business, the main thing is the *profit*, not the process, whatever that may be. If a grocer can make more money from selling his shop than he can from selling his groceries, he should sell his shop. Similarly, a shoe manufacturer should sell his factory if he can get more for it than he can from selling shoes.

We are all too apt to hold fast to our properties. We nail them down. We think of them as though they were entailed and could not be sold. Take a specific case. A young man started a sweet shop. He bought over a shop that had gone bankrupt; he bought it for a song and invested £2,500 in stocks. He is a very able and sociable young man. Everyone likes him. He has built up his business and is making £250 a week from his sweet shop. Recently, he was offered £6,000 for his shop. He refused. That was a mistake. He should have taken his profit.

During the year, he had made a profit of about £3,000. If he had sold out for £6,000, he would have made a profit of £2,500. Total profit for the year: £5,500. Then, with £6,000 in hand, he could have bought another bankrupt business - a larger one - and repeated the process; kept building them up quickly and selling them. In ten years, he could be rich. To make £2,500 in his business, he has to work hard for about ten months. He has to wait on more than 20,000 people. But to make £2,500 from selling his shop, he does not have to do any work at all - merely spend two or three days in reading and signing papers, and the deed is done.

"Ah, but," you say, "he will then have no shop. He must think what to do next."

Of course. That is why people do not sell out and take their profit. They must think. Nine out of ten would sooner drift along and make a bare living, than *think* and get rich. But, as this book is published for the Thinkers, not for the Drifters, I am pointing out a quicker and better way to make more money.

Money-making has a technique of its own, which I am trying to explain. And very frequently, you can make more money by doing something special than by conducting your business in the same old way. We could, most of us, get rich if we lived 1,000 years, but the difficulty lies in making money more quickly. We have only 20 to 30 years in which to make our fortunes.

A friend of mine wrote to me recently: "I have always been

22

able to make money happily, but I can't make *enough*." That's the point. To make enough money quickly you must take short cuts. You must snatch at every honourable chance to make a profit.

Take another instance. A London businessman bought 1,000 shares at £18 each. In six months they had risen to £23. He could have sold out and made a net profit of £5,000. But he refused to sell. He said, "No, I'll wait till they get to £28. Then I'll make twice as much." The shares then dropped again to £20. He had lost his chance. No doubt they will eventually go up to £28, but he may have to wait a long time. He would have been wiser to have taken his profit of £5,000.

If I bought a cow for £200 and if, while I was driving her to my meadow, a friend met me and said, "That's a fine cow; I'll give you £300 for her", I would say, "She's yours." Then I would go home well pleased with a well-spent afternoon. Too many people are suspicious when they are offered a high price. They think: "If it is worth as much as that to him, it is worth it to me." But this is the wrong attitude. The point is that you must take every opportunity to make a quick, sure profit.

You must consider the time element. It is better to make £100 in a month than to make £200 in a year. Once you get this clearly in your mind, you are on your way to becoming a financier. You have learned to make money by initiative, by thinking, by planning, by taking advantage of the swing of values.

Immature people regard this as exploitation. But it is nothing of the kind. It is creative energy. It is leadership. It is legitimate money-making, which is the most helpful and least destructive of all the activities of mankind.

To make money, you must be quick. You must be flexible, not rigid in your way of doing things. You must move, act, decide and take chances. And when an opportunity to make a profit comes your way, you must pounce on it. There is the old story of the silly fisherman who caught a fish a foot long. He threw it back in the water and said, "I'll come back and get you next year." Better keep what you catch. Often, by expecting too much, you will lose what you already have.

Many people have held onto their properties for 30 years and then sold them for prices they could have had in the beginning. It is better to make small profits quickly than to make a big profit eventually. "Eventually" is an uncertain word for transient creatures like us, whose average lifespan is not much more than 65 brief years.

Life is short, the future uncertain. Therefore, do not waste any opportunities that come your way now. Be quick to cash in. Every little bit added to what you already have, makes for just one little bit more in the kitty. So, take your profit.

Tip No. 6

Ask Your Banker

There are no maps and no paths in the jungle of finance. Everyone is more or less lost, most of the time. But there are a few people who have spent their lives in the jungle of finance and know the signs and dangers. Of these people, the most reliable are the bankers.

The jungle of finance, as you will find out if you venture into it, is full of would-be guides in the form of brokers, promoters and common swindlers who will offer you maps and guide-books. They will offer to guide you anywhere and tell you anything you want to know. In fact, as soon as you enter the jungle with a wallet bulging with money, you are liable to be overwhelmed with offers to take you to the Golden Mountain. Ironically, most of these so-called expert guides are themselves hopelessly lost. This is one of the weirdest customs of the jungle of finance, that sickly people offer to show you the road to health and ragged rascals offer to make you rich.

There is practically no such thing as disinterested advice or service in the jungle of finance. You would be better off knowing this before you enter the jungle. As soon as you lose your money, all the guides and advisers will disappear and you will find yourself on your own. It is then - when you are lost in the jungle - that you might be tempted to become a guide yourself. Why not make money out of others now that you have lost your own money?

If these know-all guides or brokers really knew the way to the Golden Mountain, do you think they would be foolish enough to take anyone else there for a small fee? Of course not! If you want reliable advice, the last person to go to is a broker. This is true in general and if you have any doubts about it, ask anyone who has been buying and selling shares for 20 years. It is not that brokers are dishonest, but they have a code of their own - a sort of "Ten Commandments", the first of which is: "Let the client take the risk."

They don't believe in safety. They only think in terms of action. "Go on," they will advise you. No matter where, but "just keep on going". Brokers keep everyone in the jungle moving. This, mind you, is a very valuable service to the people in the jungle as a whole. But I am not talking generalities. I am trying to tell my readers how to hold on to their money and make it earn more. No broker lies awake at night thinking of old-time clients who have lost their money. If brokers did this, they would all have died of insomnia a long time ago - no doubt about it!

Brokers rely more on rumours than on principles. They trot up and down with the market. They seldom study national tendencies, but merely follow the clients whom they are supposed to lead. They are not really guides but companions. Once you realise this, you can make very good use of a broker.

They can run errands for you, cheer you up, tell you the news of the day and buy and sell for you.

There is another class of people in the jungle who do not pretend to be guides but who know much more than the brokers. They are the bankers. These are the custodians who protect their clients' money from being lost. They are all for safety. If they do not know all the paths in the jungle of finance, at least they know the hiding places. They spend their lives studying everything pertaining to money and looking out for signs of danger. More than this, bankers can get you out of trouble if they want to. This is where they are vastly superior to brokers.

The main aim of brokers is to keep their clients buying and selling. But bankers concern themselves with protecting their clients against loss. A broker is paid by commission, on what his client buys or sells; but a banker is paid a salary.

If brokers were paid a salary, and bankers were put on commission, the whole world of finance would be marvellously altered, and whether for better or for worse, no one knows. But one thing is clear: a banker is in a better position to give disinterested advice than anybody else is.

Very few depositors make full use of their bankers. In my own early days, I had a bank account for ten years before I asked for a loan; and it was 14 years before I asked my banker's advice about investments. In those early days, I went for advice to a broker and a house agent. The former made me lose £2,500 and the latter made me lose £12,000. That is what it cost me to learn never to go for advice to anyone who is paid on commission.

When you go to your banker for advice, you help yourself in two ways:

1. You are likely to be advised wisely.
2. You improve the banker's opinion of you and thus strengthen your credit.

A banker is a sort of onlooker in the jungle of finance. He has no reason to deceive either himself or his clients. He is more of a student than a busybody, and he knows too much about the jungle to call himself a guide.

He can't tell you how to make 12 per cent, but he can tell you how to make 6 per cent. He can't tell you how to double your money, but he can tell you how to hold fast to what you have. He can't tell you the path to the Golden Mountain, although he knows that every now and then some people, by luck or by merit, find it and become fabulously rich.

A banker always plays safe, and for that reason he is the best possible adviser to every investor in the beginning. There may come a time when one has become knowledgeable enough about the jungle to outgrow his banker's advice, but that is not often.

So, our sixth Tip is - Ask your banker. Don't rely upon your own limited experience or upon the advice of anyone who may make a profit out of your losses.

Tip No. 7

Buy at the Bottom; Sell at the Top

There are only eight words in this Tip, but you could make a fortune if you could put it into action. However, few people have the courage and foresight to do this. Almost everyone buys when the crowd buys and sells when the crowd sells. Even the Stock Exchange and the Money Market are run on mob lines. Not even speculators and bankers do their own thinking.

There are always two groups in the investment market - one comprising buyers and the other, sellers. And when people enter this market, they invariably join the group that happens to be bigger at the time. This is one of the main reasons for their losing money.

Almost all of us are dominated by the herd instinct. We follow the crowd, preferably the biggest crowd, just as an ox or an elephant follows the herd. We do what others do because it is easier and more pleasant. We do not want to be thought of as odd or unfriendly. In other words, we drift. We do in finance exactly what we do in politics, religion and at other times when we are required to take a stand on important issues.

We are passive. We allow ourselves to be pushed here and there by everyone, including the Press - most of all by the

Press, which usually creates the crowds. Editors and journalists do not do more thinking than people in other professions, but what they do is far more effective - they sell their talk. Whether or not they know anything is immaterial - they must say something everyday. This incessant and emphatic talking influences their readers because most people hardly try, or can't be bothered, to analyse what they read.

Most people go from the cradle to the grave without ever doing anything alone. All their lives they are following some crowd or other. They have the general idea that it is safer to follow the crowd. This may be true in politics and for social customs, but it should not be done in finance. In finance, the crowd always loses. Only a few people win, and they do it by following values, not by following the crowd. Few people are aware of this. Those who do know keep it to themselves.

Finance is the exact opposite of politics. It cares little about the vote of the majority. Values are not made by votes.

At the same time, it is quite true that public opinion pushes prices up or down. When 20 people want to sell the shares of a certain company, and only five people want to buy, the price goes down. And when 20 people want to buy, and only five want to sell, the price goes up. But a wise investor does not buy when the crowd buys and sell when the crowd sells. The wise investor stands apart and takes advantage of price movements.

In politics, go with the biggest crowd and you will win; but in finance, you must go with the small crowd if you want to learn the difficult art of Investment and Speculation. Never buy when there are more buyers than sellers, or you are sure to pay too much. Never sell when there are more sellers than buyers, or you are sure to get too little. As one millionaire once told me: "Buy your straw hats in winter."

Buy when it's the fashion to sell, and sell when it's the fashion to buy. Prices are always moving up or down in waves. There are always booms and depressions; every boom is followed by a depression and every depression is followed by a boom.

The crowd, of course, never looks ahead. The crowd is always foolish. It thinks only of the present moment. That is why most people buy when prices are high and sell when prices are low. They think that present conditions will last forever. Most people are optimists during a boom and pessimists during a depression. But the ones who make money are those who are pessimists during a boom and optimists during a depression.

Always buy from pessimists. Always sell to optimists. This is the seventh Tip, put in another form. It means that you will stand apart from the crowd and take advantage of price fluctuations. The few people who have the courage to do this get rich, and they deserve all that they get. They are the steadiers of the market. They prevent the crowd from stampeding and smashing things. That is what all crowds usually do. Take away the independent speculators from any Stock Exchange, and that Stock Exchange would be closed in a year. It would be smashed by either a boom or a depression.

It is an odd quirk of human nature, that when prices are high, we think they are likely to go higher; and when they are low, we think they are likely to go even lower. Of course, the reverse is the truth. Whatever is high is apt to fall, and whatever is low is apt to rise. Prices may move above or below the line of value, but they seldom go out of sight in either direction. Eventually they will stabilise.

Tip No. 8

Keep Your Money Moving

The most efficient capitalist in the world is perhaps the news paper seller. He can make a 100 per cent profit a day. How? By keeping his money and his goods moving.

Let's say he starts with a capital of £8 and buys 20 papers at 40 pence a copy. He sells them at 50 pence a copy and gets £10. He repeats this process three times more during the day and ends up making a profit of £8 after selling 80 copies.

He is the best illustration of the importance of keeping money and goods rolling. He makes nearly £3,000 a year on his original investment of £8, plus a great deal of hard work. Compare him with a jeweller, who has a £500,000 stock of jewellery, and whose sales are £500,000 a year. The newspaper seller turns his money over hundreds of times, while the jeweller only turns his money over once.

This brings us to a great law of finance - it is not the amount of your capital that matters as much as the activity. Does your capital move once a year, or once a quarter, or once a month, or once a week?

I know of two firms situated side by side. One has a capital of £18,000,000 and 18,000 employees and the other, a capital of

£1,800,000 and 800 employees. In one year, each of these firms made the same amount of profit. This is partly because the smaller firm was more efficient, partly because it turned its money over 26 times in the year.

A baker can do a good business on one-tenth as much capital as a jeweller. He can do this because he turns his flour into bread and his bread into money so quickly. He practically sells out his whole stock in a day.

One of the universal reasons why most companies make such small profits is that they have too much money tied up. Too many goods on the high shelves! Too many machines not working! Too much raw material! Too many buildings! All this means idle capital. It is a sort of paralysis. Often, two-thirds of a company's capital lies idle while the other third has to bear the whole load.

There is no profit to be made out of the possession of goods, unless prices are rising. The value of a machine or a building depends on its use, not on its cost. The business world is full of white elephants - expensive things that do not make any money.

It is better to have a small van that is being used throughout the day than a huge truck that is left idle. It is better to have £2,000 of stock that's moving than to have £20,000 tied up in dead stock. The essence of business is exchange. Money for goods - goods for money - money for goods again! And quickly - that is the secret of big dividends.

Take a case of two furniture dealers - one slow and one fast.

Each buys £200 worth of chairs. The slow one keeps the chairs a year and sells them for £300. The fast one sells them in three months for £250. He buys more chairs and sells these in the next three months for £310. He buys again and sells for £370. He buys again and sells for £450. At the end of the year, the slow dealer has made £100, but he has charged his customers a high price and will probably lose their trade. The fast dealer has made £250 at the end of the year. He has paid his sales people more and he has charged his customers less.

Here you have, in a few words, the reason why one shop doubles its trade while another shop, alongside of it, can barely hold its own. The fast dealer probably spent £50 on advertising his chairs; but, even then, he charged 25 per cent less than the slow dealer and made 100 per cent more profits. The slow dealer marked his goods up 50 per cent, yet he only made half as much profit as the fast dealer, who marked his goods up only 25 per cent.

Your rate of profit depends more upon quick selling than on high prices. It is more profitable to make five per cent a month than to make 30 per cent a year. Moneylenders know this, but very few business people do. That is why so many business people have dead stock and a live overdraft.

Money is like brains. It was formerly believed that the bigger a person's brain, the wiser he would be, but we know now that this is not always true. A person may have a very big brain, but if it is slow and sluggish, he is stupid. The main thing in a brain is not size but activity.

Invariably, when I ask business people what they need most, they reply, "more capital". Generally speaking, they are quite wrong. What they need is to make quicker use of the capital they have. People can double their capital without borrowing anything by merely turning over their goods twice as fast.

It is better to study salesmanship than to pay interest. It is cheaper to advertise than to have a big overdraft. The golden rule is: "In - out. In today - out tomorrow." And this rule holds good for financiers as well as business people.

Don't over-buy. Don't over-build. Always have more customers than goods and more business than buildings. It is better to turn a customer away than to carry goods over. A shop is a temporary depot, not a warehouse - how few are the business people who know this!

Keep your money moving. Every pound is a little "worker" and you must put it to work, not to sleep, so that it will get busy and come back to you in a few weeks, leading a new pound by the hand.

Tip No. 9

Borrow All You Can Use

Dare to borrow. This is one thing that most people in business should not be afraid to do.

Most of them have a horror of debt. They keep their companies on a cash basis. They play safe. They sail upon the ocean of trade and commerce with a small boat called "cash" and keep close to the shore - so close that their boats run aground on the rocks and that is the end of their businesses. Later in life, they learn that most rocks are near the shore, and that it is safer to navigate in deep waters.

If you want to play safe and avoid risks, you will never be a financier, unless you are born one. You may be able to keep the money your father made, but you will never make much of your own. You might as well tell a lion-hunter to play safe, as caution a financier. You might as well tell a racing-driver not to run any risks.

The world of finance is full of risks, and no one can tell you how to avoid all of them. An old lion-hunter could give valuable tips to a young hunter; but every lion-hunter has scars on his body, make no mistake about that. Nothing is more profitable in the long run than a business risk taken wisely. Ask Lloyds. Ask any insurance company. But one must have enough courage. One must enjoy the adventure of a risk.

A person who lies awake at night, worrying about a debt, should never be a financier. He should remain an employee, in a safe, salaried job. But those people who are prepared to take the risk and who have shown that they are capable of handling other people's money should proceed to borrow as much money as they can. Andrew Carnegie, the man who made a £60,000,000 fortune in the steel business, borrowed every penny he could get when he started in business. "I was the biggest borrower in Pennsylvania," he said. "I kept one of my partners going from bank to bank, borrowing all he could get."

Successful business people will tell you that they owe a great deal of their success to money which they borrowed for a wise purpose. A few companies, but not many, have financed themselves entirely out of their own profits. But that is not finance. That is merchandising - quite a different thing.

Recently, I met a businessman who told me that he had been in business for 27 years and had never borrowed a penny. He was proud of it. He had a small factory with fifty employees. His net income was probably £15,000 at the most. This was well enough, but the point is that he had taken 27 years to build his business up to the £15,000 mark. If he had borrowed £50,000 in the beginning, he could have built up his business in at least a quarter of the time. He had forgotten the time element. He had taken a lifetime to do what he might have done in five years.

There is nothing so cheap as money. I go to a factory, for instance, and I find three men shovelling coal. They are paid £100 a week apiece. This is £5,200 a year. If I hired money, instead of labour, with this £5,200 I could borrow £86,666 at 6 per cent. But I could put in machinery to do the work of these three men, for £60,000. Consequently, it would save £26,000 of capital to borrow money instead of hiring labour. Every worker who gets £100 a week represents a capital outlay of £86,666.

There is very little net profit to be made by hiring labour. Take labour as a whole and you will find that it does not earn its own wages. It is machinery that makes the profit - machinery and salesmanship and management and advertising and personal leadership. Money and brains - they make the profit in every line of business.

Labour has pushed up its own wages, without pushing up its own productivity - there you have the basic reason why there are so many unemployed. The only profitable way to employ people these days is to have them operate machines which you buy with money. The machine will then pay for itself. It will pay the man's wages and make a small profit besides.

Money means machinery and equipment and advertising and mass production. Money puts the profit-making factors into a business - all of them except brains. Consequently, my advice is: once you are sure that you have brains, in a business sense, your next step should be to get money. If you can get it without borrowing, that is best of all; but if not, then you must borrow it.

From whom? Not from moneylenders. You should never go near a moneylender, unless you are friendless and in a most desperate plight. You can never make any profit out of money borrowed from a moneylender, for the simple reason that you are usually obliged to pay anything from 10 to 30 per cent interest a month. Moreover, a moneylender's office is apt to be a trap, in which every possible penny is squeezed out of its victims.

No, you must get your money as cheaply as possible. Don't pay seven per cent if you can get enough money for six. It makes a difference of £100 a year on every £10,000. Get your money from a bank, if you can. A bank's business is lending money, and a bank will most probably give you better terms and be more merciful in a hard year than any friend or relative will.

Banks are generally supposed to be hard and heartless. The fact is that they are not. The last thing that any banker wants to do is to ruin one of his borrowers. If you cannot borrow any money from a bank, you had better take it as a sign that you should not borrow any at all. A banker is a skilled specialist on lending. He knows when to lend and when to refuse.

Certainly, you ought to acquire some money of your own first, before you consider asking other people for money. But once you have proven that you can make good use of money, it is better to borrow more than to spend a whole lifetime earning it.

If you have business acumen and want to make more money more quickly, take this ninth Tip and borrow all you can use.

Tip No. 10

Borrow for Expansion, Not for Swank

Hundreds of businesses have tumbled down into bankruptcy because they did not realise the importance of this Tip. They did not know the difference between expansion and swank.

Expansion means the growth of a business itself, while swank means hanging ornaments on the business. Expansion means increasing the size and capacity of the business at a time when it is oversold, while swank means increasing the prestige and appearance of it. If a printer finds himself losing £40,000 worth of orders a year for lack of a new press, he should borrow money and buy the press. If a jeweller finds that he could sell more diamonds if he had a larger stock, he should borrow money and buy more diamonds.

There is such a thing as the compulsion of growth. A growing business is like a growing boy. It cannot be kept in the cradle. It must have larger quarters. But swank, on the other hand, is all a matter of appearance. It is decorative. It is what we like to have, rather than what we need.

Money should never be borrowed unless it can be made to pay for itself and return a good profit beside. If you borrow £10,000 at 6 per cent, you should be able to make at least 16 per cent on it.

Many a time I have visited a struggling little shop or factory that was badly in need of more goods or machinery, and the owner took me out to lunch in an expensive car. Many a time I have felt like saying: "Better sell your car and buy some more machines." I have seen people living in fine houses with their sideboards glistening with silver, while their places of business were not even properly lit or heated. Too many people enrich themselves and impoverish their businesses. Little by little, their wives and their friends nag them into spending more and more until there is nothing left to keep the business going.

If I owned some of these people's factories that are struggling to survive, I would sell my house and sleep in my office on a couple of desks with an overcoat for a blanket and a bag of wool for a pillow. I would cook my own meals on an oil stove and put what I save into the business. Then, when I had enough assets, I would borrow all I could and put all of it straight into the business. That is the way to build up a strong, robust business that will not collapse when things get a little rough.

Sir Jesse Boot slept in his workshop when he was young. Sir Thomas Lipton slept in his grocer's shop, under the counter. Cecil Rhodes slept anywhere - in a hut or on a hill. Every great business-builder has always put his business first and himself second. Just as a great General thinks first of his men, so should you put your business first.

No money should ever be taken out of a business, if the business will miss it. It is better to forego the dividend than to cripple the business. In a word, you must be a bit of a spartan if you want to start with nothing and make a fortune in one short life-time. There is no easy way, apart from luck.

You must avoid swank in your business as well as in your own personal habits. The main thing, always and everywhere, about every business, is not its appearance but its ability to make profits. It is better to have a successful factory in a shed than have a failing one in a perfect building of steel and glass. Doubling the size of a shop-front does not double the business. In fact, it only increases the business by 30 or 40 per cent at the most.

New buildings! There you have one reason why dozens of companies fail. No doubt it is right in theory that a business should be well-housed, but the truth is that the building always matters less than we think it does. Experienced business people can tell you that a new building can become a financial embarrassment. You yourself may know of some businesses that failed recently because of the money spent on new buildings. I know of at least three manufacturers who would give a year of their lives to be out of their new buildings and back in the old ones.

Personally, I do not remember more than two occasions when I felt it was feasible to construct new buildings. More often than not, I have found that companies do not make the best possible use of the buildings they now occupy. So, why waste time, energy and money putting up new buildings?

A new building may be needed for expansion. If so, build it, but make sure that it is not for swank. This is one of the commonest mistakes in some countries - to overwhelm a business with style. Many a company has put up a grand, new building, only to find out soon enough that it becomes a mausoleum for a dead business.

There is such a thing, too, as spending too much money on lavish, expensive furnishings for offices, especially for the upper echelons of the company. All this is superstructure. It adds to the expenses but does nothing to boost profits. Every business, as it grows, is in danger of becoming ornamental at the top. Every business accumulates extras - both human and mechanical; and no money should be borrowed to pay for these extras.

All borrowed money must be productive. If not, it does more harm than good, as it introduces habits of self-indulgence. There are two motives in business - profit and pride. If you borrow for profit, all is well. But if you borrow for pride, then your business is in danger. Borrowed money either lifts you or crushes you, according to the use you make of it. That is why you should always borrow for expansion but never for swank.

Tip No. 11

Give, But Never Lend

At the risk of being called hardhearted, I am going to say a few things that need to be said about the danger of lending money to friends. It would have saved me quite a bit of money and half a dozen friends if someone had told me these things 30 years ago. The fact is that as soon as you are known to have money, you will find yourself with a new set of problems. This is when the parasites turn up.

An encyclopaedia could be compiled about these parasites. They range from the half-drunken whiners at the kerb to bishops in their elaborate robes. They can be relatives, friends or strangers, women as well as men, the honest and the dishonest, the deserving and the worthless. All have one thing in common - they want your money, make no mistake about that.

Parasites all! Beautiful women with saintly faces. Dignified gentlemen with the manners of courtiers. Nephews and nieces, uncles and aunts. All with their hands out and their eyes on your pocket. There is no sure way of detecting parasites until the revealing moment comes, when they suggest that you should transfer some of your money from your pocket to theirs. There is no easy way of escaping from either the respectable beggars or the disreputable ones. Many business people have had the shock of their lives to discover that even their own children have the instincts of a beggar!

There is a constant war going on between the builders and the beggars in this world. The beggars overthrew the Roman Empire and they have now become so strong in many countries that no one can tell how the fight will end. Every person in business who is a builder is surrounded by beggars, just as a lion in the jungle has jackals hanging around, waiting for the chance to dart in and steal its food. Happy is the builder who marries a woman who also has the spirit of a builder. He is sure to be a success. But, as for the builder who marries a beggar, God pity him! No matter how strong and clever he is, he will be pulled down in the end.

It is as hard to keep money as it is to get it - every wealthy person knows that. That is why rich people, as a rule, are so cautious. They are compelled to be always on their guard. They almost develop quills, like a hedgehog. And no wonder!

Builders must protect themselves against beggars - that is the meaning of the eleventh Tip. As soon as you have any money in the bank, you must learn to say "No". This does not mean that you are being hardhearted. No matter how big your fortune is, it can be taken away from you in a very short time, if you are not on your guard. I once knew a man named De Bardeleben who discovered an iron mine and sold it for £500,000. He went to New York and in six weeks he had lost every penny of it. There is no limit to the rapacity of the parasites. The more you lend, the more they want.

They are insatiable.

If you have a small fortune and want to keep it, there are some rules you must follow:

1. You must keep your capital intact. Whatever you give or lend must come out of your income.

2. You must not endorse another person's note, no matter who the person may be.

3. You must not sign any blank cheques.

4. You must not have a joint banking account with anyone, not even with your spouse.

5. You must keep out of all money entanglements, for there is nothing that brings out the worst in most people like a difference of opinion about money.

Leave lending to bankers and pawnbrokers. They know how. You don't. They have the means of protecting themselves. You don't. It is worth noting that professional moneylenders usually charge at least 10 to 30 per cent interest a month. Very likely they are obliged to do this to make up for their many losses and their high operating expenses.

Lending is a half-way thing. It is neither giving nor investing. It does not bring you any thanks nor give you any chance of a profit. It is worse than betting, for there is no excitement in it, no sport, no possibility of good luck. If a friend of yours tries to borrow money from you, first ask him why he does not go to a banker. Then, when he confesses to you that he is in a hole, don't lend him the money. Do better than that. Buy a small interest in his business - enough to set him on his feet again.

It is always better to invest than to lend. If you become a shareholder, then you have a right to advise and a right to a share in the profits. If your friend succeeds, you will have a share in his success, not merely six per cent; and if he fails, you will get at least a part of your money back.

As a rule, people who borrow from friends are generally unreliable and often parasitical. They are like clinging ivy. Self-reliant, independent people will not let their friends know that they need money. To put it bluntly, the person who asks for money is not likely to deserve it, while the person who deserves it won't ask for it.

People of the clinging-ivy type can be found in all towns and cities. They are without a conscience in the matter of debts. They take life easy - and anything else they can lay their hands on without doing a stroke of work.

They may be well-educated and charming but they are mendicants. They beg for "fivers" and cigars and weekends. They are merely gilded loafers who deserve no consideration from self-respecting people. Such parasites lack the courage to become thieves. They keep within the law. But they take more money from other people than thieves do.

A curious thing about lending is that when you lend money to honest people, you are apt to lose their friendship. No one has yet written a book on the psychology of ingratitude, but it is a very interesting subject and deserves to be considered.

No one likes a moneylender. This is strange but true. As soon as you lend a friend money, you cease to be a pal and become a Shylock. Your friend is likely to think of the debt as a burden, and will blame you for putting that burden on him. This is stupid and illogical, but it is what happens in the minds of most people.

Friendship depends on equality and reciprocity. It is destroyed by philanthropy. If I take a friend to a restaurant twice and if I pay both times, our friendship is in danger. Friendship cannot exist between superiors and inferiors. This is a law of human nature that cannot be ignored.

Speaking on a moral plane, you do people a disservice if you lend them money just because they ask for it. You weaken their self-reliance and self-respect. If they ask for money, they evidently need far more than money - make no mistake about that.

We lend too often but we don't give often enough. We should give more often, and we should give only to people who are doing their best to help themselves.

Tip No. 12

Buy the Ordinary Shares of the Best Company in the Worst Trade.

This one Tip is worth the lot, for those who can understand it and use it. For years I have found it quite as good as receiving a pension, and much more exciting.

Not only will this Tip make money for those who dare use it, but it will render a public service as well, by preventing slumps and booms from going too far either way. There is almost always some trade or industry that is undergoing a slump. It may be coffee or rubber or tin or cotton. Invariably, there is at least one company in that trade or industry that is known to be safe, progressive and well-financed - a company with a big reserve. This company must have ordinary shares. It is better to buy ordinary shares because they rise higher and fall lower than other securities.

In a trade slump, the best company in the trade will be pulled down with the rest. Its ordinary shares will drop drastically. So, if you buy the ordinary shares of the best company in a depressed trade, you are as sure of a profit as anyone can be sure of anything in this world of risks. This is because you are betting on the trade rather than on one company. No trade remains always on the downturn. All trades have their ups and downs, and when the trade begins to pick up, your shares will be the first to rise.

This Tip, of course, is only for those who have the money and the nerve to speculate in the securities of the Stock Exchange. I am not at all alarmed that too many people will immediately proceed to try out this Tip. If a lion-hunter revealed his secret for killing lions, there would not likely be any great rush to the jungle.

Knowledge by itself is of little use to anyone. It is knowledge in action that achieves results, and not many people are people of action. If I were writing for a daily paper, I would say, "Keep your savings in the savings bank. Take your five per-cent and be content."

But I am writing these Tips for the Efficient Few; and my purpose is to enable them to make more money more quickly, more easily and more happily. My whole purpose in life, in these later years, is to train as many money-makers as possible - and to enable honest men to hold their own against rogues.

Consequently, I am bringing this series of Tips to an end with a grande finale, by giving my own personal system of specu-lation. Bear in mind that it is my system, not yours. If you try it and lose money, that only means that you had better get a system of your own and let mine alone.

Usually, when I am asked to give advice on Stock Exchange securities, I say:

If you want safety, buy Debentures;

If you want speculation, buy Preference;

If you want sport, buy Ordinary.

But this twelfth Tip is, as you can see, more than just a Tip. It is a definite, reasonable way of making money by taking advantage of the rise and fall in Stock Exchange prices.

The Stock Exchange is one of the most useful and wonderful institutions in the world. It is the high-water mark of financial civilisation. Fools dislike it and weaklings fear it. Both have good reason to do so; it is not intended for fools or weaklings. "Keep away from the Stock Exchange," say these people. "It is a place of robbery." They might as well say, "Keep away from Hyde Park Corner. It is a place of death. Nine people were run over and killed there last year."

True, the Stock Exchange, like Hyde Park Corner, has its dangers and its accidents. But the remedy does not lie in destroying either place. The remedy lies in being as careful as possible and in keeping children and weaklings away. There are some places reserved for the strong, and the weak should stay clear of them. One of these places is the Stock Exchange.

The Stock Exchange is a marketplace where you can at once either buy or sell securities. On the London Stock Exchange, there are seven thousand securities listed with a value of £1.862 billion, that you can either buy or sell. The Stock Exchange is as necessary as the railroads, the docks and the airport. If it were destroyed today, another one would spring up tomorrow to take its place. It is more than a market, too. It is a barometer of trade and commerce. Everyone in business should read one of the financial dailies and study the stock market.

The Stock Exchange looks ahead. It gets all the news first. It is always in advance. Stock Exchange prices do not represent value. They represent the tendencies and outlook of the day. They represent public opinion. No individual is wiser or stronger than the Stock Exchange. No individual can make artificial prices, as the novelists say they do. Now and then, some speculator with a swollen head tries to play tricks with prices, but the market opens up and swallows him. Prices are moved by facts and fancies, fears and rumours, wishes and excitements. Crops, weather, strikes, wars, elections, the Bank rate, the Budget - all these push prices up or down.

There is often a great difference between the price of a stock and its real value. The most successful speculators are those who are the most indifferent to public opinion and most aware of real values. As a further help in following this Tip, I would suggest the following procedure:

1. Select 15 to 20 securities.

2. Select those of which you have some personal knowledge.

3. Select those in your own town or city, to begin with.

4. Select only those securities that are frequently bought and sold on the Stock Exchange.

5. Select securities that are at least five years old.

6. Select securities of companies that are well-managed and widely known.

7. Select securities from at least a dozen different trades.

8. Select domestic, not foreign securities, unless you live in a country with serious problems.

Then, when you have made your list, watch the movement of prices. When there is a slump in one of the trades, you will notice that the ordinary shares of one of your selected firms are depressed. When this happens, give the order to buy, and at the same time, give your stockbroker an order to sell at a 25 per cent rise. Then forget the whole matter until they are sold. This comes as near to scientific, safe and automatic speculation as anyone can expect.

If anyone knows of "a better 'ole", let him go to it. This is the one that I have dug for myself after 30 years' experience in speculation and that I am now offering to you.